Serving the Master

A Catholic Bible Study
on Stewardship

By Rich Cleveland

Emmaus Journey is an evangelization and discipleship ministry of
The Navigators, an interdenominational religious organization, conducted in and
through Catholic parishes.

The Word Among Us Press
9639 Doctor Perry Road
Ijamsville, Maryland 21754
www.wordamongus.org

Theological advisor: Rev. Alfredo I. Hernandez, S.T.L.

ISBN 1-59325-014-2

Made and printed in the United States of America

Cover images:Duccio (c.1260-1318)
Christ Appearing to the Apostles on the Lake of Tiberias
Scala/Art Resource, NY

Library of Congress Control Number: 2003109312

Acknowledgments

I wish to acknowledge the dedicated help and partnership of my wife, Gail Cleveland, in the development of these materials. We are also appreciative of the welcoming environment presented by Father Paul Wicker and Holy Apostles Catholic Church. Many individuals freely shared their insights as participants or as leaders of the small groups in which these materials were developed. We are grateful for their help.

Acknowledgments continue on page 96.

Table of Contents

Introduction 7

Session 1
The Foundation of Being a Disciple of Jesus 10

Session 2
God's Trustworthy Steward 22

Session 3
Jesus' Responsible Servant 30

Session 4
Stewardship of Our Hearts 38

Session 5
Yielding Our Hearts to God 50

Session 6
The Way in Which We Live: 60
Our Time and Our Work

Session 7
The Way in Which We Live: 70
Our Finances and Our Words

Session 8
Entrusted with Jesus' Mission 80

Session 9
Ambassadors for Christ 90

Paul described the transformation that took place in the lives of the Thessalonian Christians when he said they "turned to God from idols, to serve the living and true God, and to wait for his Son from heaven" (1 Thessalonians 1:9-10). What Paul was writing about is a transformation that should take place in the lives of all of us as baptized Catholic believers—a transformation that we often refer to as discipleship.

Pope Paul VI spoke about it in this way: "This kingdom and this salvation … are available to every human being as grace and mercy. . . . Each individual gains them through a total interior renewal which the Gospel calls *metanoia;* it is a radical conversion, a profound change of mind and heart" (*Evangelii Nuntiandi*, 10). Pope John Paul II echoed this belief when he explained that "Conversion is expressed in faith which is total and radical. . . . At the same time it gives rise to a dynamic and lifelong process which demands a continual turning away from 'life according to the flesh' to 'life according to the Spirit'" (*Mission of the Redeemer*, 46).

These phrases—"turned to God from idols, to serve the living and true God," "a total interior renewal," "a profound change of mind and heart," and "a dynamic and lifelong process"—are terms which reflect what *Serving the Master* is all about. It is about issues of discipleship and stewardship and what it means practically to live out our baptism as followers of Christ.

Our prayer for you as you venture into this study is that God will give you this radical willingness to change and that you will experience the joy that comes from serving the Master with all of your being.

Sincerely,
Fr. Sean Wenger, Pastor
St. Thomas Aquinas Church
Halifax, Nova Scotia
Canada

Introduction

Jesus began his ministry by devoting a night to prayer. The next day he called twelve ordinary men to come and be his disciples. In the subsequent months he taught them about the Father's love and truth. This began a transformation process that ultimately enabled them to live as productive citizens in God's kingdom. After Jesus' Passion, he entrusted his disciples with the mission of spreading the Good News by their words and deeds throughout the world. Jesus ascended to the Father with this strategy in place; he offered no other.

Today that strategy has not changed. Jesus still offers only one plan. He still desires that the world might know and experience the Father's love. He is still relying on faithful, obedient, and yet very ordinary disciples to spread the Good News by their words and deeds. He is still calling people to follow him. By the transforming power of the Holy Spirit, he is still entrusting the mission to faithful stewards.

This study will help you to look afresh at Jesus' call, to consider anew his teachings, and to affirm once again—or perhaps for the first time— your willingness to be his faithful disciple and steward. As you begin, plan on setting aside at least one hour to work through each session. Come with an open heart and mind as you explore the issues raised within these pages. During the course of the Bible study, if the Lord shows you an area in your life that needs changing, be open to change so that you can carry on Jesus' mission in the world today.

Serving the Master: A Catholic Bible Study on Stewardship was developed and field-tested through the Small Christian Communities ministry of Holy Apostles Catholic Church in Colorado Springs, Colorado, so it lends itself to use in small groups. However, it can also be used individually or with a spouse or friend. If you are part of a faith-sharing group, plan on spending another hour or two together discussing your journey. If you are new to a faith-sharing group, here are some helpful attitudes to keep in mind:

1. **Preparation.** The Bible study discussion is built on the premise that each person has invested the necessary time to think about the passages and answer the questions. To be unprepared turns the Bible study discussions into a sharing of opinions. Though you may not be able to prepare every time, to choose not to prepare deprives the group of the blessings of God working in your life. Selecting a specific time to do your study each week and establishing a consistent place to study can help you be prepared.

2. **Teachability.** Try to be open to discovering new truths and looking at old truths in a new way. We always learn more as we open ourselves up to new concepts.

3. **Wholeheartedness.** There may be days when you feel too emotionally and spiritually down to participate in the Bible discussion. While it is helpful to acknowledge these feelings, giving in to them can negatively affect the whole group's experience. God can use the discussion and community experiences to lift your spirit. Try to participate enthusiastically even when you don't feel like it.

4. **Willingness to Apply What You've Learned.** The purpose of a Bible study is to change lives, which means changing our attitudes and behaviors. The process of bringing new attitudes and behaviors to life is stifled when we close ourselves off to the attitudes and behavior changes we feel God is asking of us. On the other hand, when we apply the truths we've discovered in the Scriptures, our lives can change dramatically. These will grow into mature values as we continue to follow Christ.

5. **Respect for All Contributions and Contributors to the Discussion.** Each of the members of your group will approach the study from different backgrounds and different ways of thinking. Each person has a valuable contribution to make. It is important to listen and learn from one another.

Facilitator's Guide. A special guide is available for leaders of small groups. It includes suggestions for handling the various sessions and for creating and sustaining positive small-group dynamics. This guide can be downloaded for free at www.emmausjourney.org.

I pray that through this Bible study, your love for the Lord will increase and your commitment to serve the master will be strengthened and renewed.

Rich Cleveland

Session 1

The Foundation of Being a Disciple of Jesus

▶ Before You Begin

Get acquainted with the others in your group by sharing your answers to these questions:
• What is your name?
• What is your favorite dessert?
• What one item do you own that best expresses who you are?

How do we live a life centered on Jesus Christ? What essentials are necessary? For centuries, Christians have asked these questions. Some have imagined our life in Christ as a wheel, with Christ as its center. Our lives, which revolve around Christ, are represented by the rim of the wheel. The sacraments, sacred Scripture, and prayer are essential ways by which Christ communicates his life and graces to us, and are represented by the vertical spokes. The horizontal spokes represent the Church's communication to others through community and evangelization. Pope John Paul II used the illustration of the cross to explain this twofold dimension of our Christian life, referring to the vertical dimension of the cross as our relationship with God, and the horizontal dimension of the cross as our relationships with others in the human family (*Reconciliation and Penance*, 7).

As individual members of the Church, we can participate in this mission of evangelization both by the witness of our words and through corporal works of mercy. As we begin this Bible study on becoming disciples of Jesus and stewards of his gospel, we can use these images of a wheel and a cross to discuss what it means to be a true follower of the Lord.

The Rim

The follower of Christ comes into daily contact with many people each day. The rim of the wheel represents our interactions with others. The quality of our lives in Christ affects both the impression others have of us and our potential impact on them.

1. (a) According to Matthew 5:13-16, what do you think it means to be "salt and light" to the people around us?

    Salt - be the food of the earth

    Light - be a light for Jesus by example

    (b) How would you describe the characteristics and effects of salt, light, and good works?

Christ at the Center

It can be demanding to relate to people as salt and light and to continually give ourselves to others through good deeds. The person who attempts to do so by his own strength and without the right motives may end up either self-righteous and proud, or discouraged and burned out. *It is vital that the love of Christ become the power source at the center of our lives.* This power comes from experiencing and knowing God's love for us through Christ, and by developing and expressing a sincere and pure devotion to God. There are many ways we can grow in our faith, love, and obedience to Christ. One important way is to nurture a heart of gratitude and love for Christ and his sacrifice by regularly attending Mass and receiving the Eucharist.

The Eucharist is "the source and summit of the Christian life" (Vatican II, *Dogmatic Constitution on the Church*, 11), and as such it "preserves, increases, and renews the life of grace received at Baptism" (*Catechism of the Catholic Church*, 1392). Thomas á Kempis explains that the Eucharist "… is the health of soul and body, the cure of every spiritual malady. By it our vices are cured, our passions restrained, temptations are lessened, grace is given in fuller measure, and virtue once established is fostered; faith is confirmed, hope is strengthened, and love kindled and deepened" (*The Imitation of Christ*, Book IV, Chapter 4).

2. Read about the disciples on the road to Emmaus (Luke 24:13-35). What two things happened that redirected them from disillusionment and despair to enthusiasm and purposefulness?

_____

_____

_____

_____

3. Paul's prayer for the Ephesians reveals the importance of understanding God's love for us. In Ephesians 3:14-21, what is the connection between the love we experience and the power we need to live for Christ?

_____

_____

_____

_____

4. In Matthew 22:36-37, Jesus says that we are to love God with all our heart, with all our soul, and with all our mind. What practical steps can we take to love God more deeply?

_____

_____

_____

_____

Means of Grace

When Christ is at the center of our lives, we can appropriate and demonstrate his power. As Pope John Paul II noted, there are two dimensions to our Christian life. The vertical dimension includes the sacraments, sacred Scripture, and prayer, which represent essential means for growing in our relationship with God. The horizontal dimension of community and personal witness represent essential means to share "Christ in us" with those we meet. These are vital elements for connecting our love for Christ, who should be the center of our existence, to the practical realities of our lives—both in our personal relationship with the Lord and in how we relate to others.

If we want Christ to remain in the center of our lives, it is important that we focus on him through sacred Scripture, prayer, and the sacraments. God uses sacred Scripture as a way to communicate with us, and prayer is one of the primary ways we can communicate with him. Regular participation in Mass and the liturgy develops a heart of affection toward Christ.

God's Word

5. Catholics believe that "Sacred Tradition and Sacred Scripture make up one sacred deposit of the word of God, which is entrusted to the Church" (Vatican II, *Dogmatic Constitution on Divine Revelation*, 10). Consequently we revere Scripture, including the words in the gospels that Jesus spoke when he walked the earth, as God's word. What does John 14:21-26 teach us about obedience and establishing a close relationship between God the Father, Jesus, and ourselves?

_____

_____

_____

_____

Prayer

6. Both the Old and New Testaments give abundant examples of the importance of prayer in the lives of believers. What is the significance of the guidance Jesus gives to his disciples prior to teaching them the Lord's Prayer (Matthew 6:5-8)?

_____

_____

_____

_____

The Sacraments

"The purpose of the sacraments is to sanctify men, to build up the Body of Christ and, finally, to give worship to God. Because they are signs they also instruct. They not only presuppose faith, but by words and objects they also nourish, strengthen, and express it" (Vatican II, _Constitution on the Sacred Liturgy_, 59). In Matthew 18:18-20, Jesus promised the Church his continuing presence and power. The Church recognizes Christ's continuing presence and power through what is referred to as the sacramental economy: "In this age of the Church Christ now lives and acts in and with his Church, in a new way appropriate to this new age . . . . through the sacraments" (CCC, 1076).

7. On the road to Emmaus (Luke 24:13-31), the disciples recognized Jesus not only in the opening of the Scriptures but also in the breaking of the bread. What does this imply about the power of the Eucharist?

_____

_____

_____

_____

If Christ is the center of our lives, and we are maintaining and growing our relationship with him through prayer, sacred Scripture, and the sacraments, we will grow increasingly concerned with those issues that concern him. Simply stated, Jesus is concerned that his message of Good News be communicated to people who do not know him, and that we who are his body live a life of love and service toward one another.

A Loving Witness

8. In 2 Corinthians 5:14-21, St. Paul establishes the tie between experiencing Christ's love within our own hearts and our calling to share Christ's love. According to this passage, what are the important elements of that relationship?

    _____

    _____

    _____

    _____

A Loving Life

9. St. John teaches that love is the distinguishing mark of a Christian (1 John 3:14-18). As you reflect on this passage, what principles do you discover for loving one another?

    _____

    _____

    _____

    _____

> If any Christian can be called upon to bear witness to his faith at any moment in his own life or in that of his community, if the Church all through her history has never been dispensed for one single day from bearing witness, is it not paradoxical that so many Christians today refuse to proclaim their faith for fear of being accused of proselytism? . . .
>
> I shall answer you briefly. The Church of our time must be conscious—and she is conscious—that her irreplaceable mission, her fundamental duty to humanity and the world is and will always everywhere remain spreading the Gospel.
>
> —**Pope John Paul II** in *"Be Not Afraid!"*, pp. 179-180

10. How do you feel about embracing this mission?

_____

_____

_____

_____

11. The image of the wheel is not designed to express *all* the ingredients of a disciple's life. What would you add? What are some additional ways we can experience God's love for us? How can we further develop our love for him? What are other ways in which the centrality of Christ will be expressed through our lives?

_____

_____

_____

_____

_____

_____

During the next eight sessions, we will consider four practical aspects of discipleship and stewardship. Christ lived, died, rose again, and gave us the Holy Spirit to create new people who live for him—not just theoretically, but practically. A practical and intangible consequence of Christ's life is that we can experience a full, new life and demonstrate hope to others. In this Bible study, we will spend two sessions each examining the following four topics: (1) responsible stewardship; (2) stewardship of the heart; (3) stewardship of life; and (4) stewardship of Christ's mission.

▶ Preparation for Session 2

1. Continue to read and mark your Bible daily, and record your thoughts in your prayer journal.

2. Complete questions 1–4 on "God's Trustworthy Steward," pages 24-27.

Notes for Session 1

Notes for Session 1

Notes for Session 1

Session 2

God's Trustworthy Steward

▶ Before You Begin

Share insights from your prayer time and daily Bible reading.

> Becoming a disciple of Jesus Christ leads naturally to the practice of stewardship. These linked realities, discipleship and stewardship, then make up the fabric of a Christian life in which each day is lived in an intimate, personal relationship with the Lord. . . .
>
> Following Jesus is the work of a lifetime. At every step forward, one is challenged to go further in accepting and loving God's will. Being a disciple is not just something else to do, alongside many other things suitable for Christians, it is a total way of life and requires continuing conversion.
>
> —*Stewardship: A Disciple's Response*, National Conference of Catholic Bishops

Discipleship and stewardship can sound more complicated to us than they really are. That's because we often emphasize the results we desire instead of the means to get there. In reality, living as a steward of the gospel is simply the natural—or should we say supernatural—response of people who have developed a deep and lasting love for Jesus. When love for Christ is at the center of our lives, we want to do the things that please him and that bring joy to our own lives because we are expressing our love for him. When not motivated by love and devotion, discipleship and stewardship become burdensome chores.

In this session we will study the general concept of stewardship. In later sessions we'll look at specific ways our stewardship can be directed. Our goal by the end of these sessions will be to recognize stewardship as an opportunity to live in harmony with God's will so that we experience its benefits in our daily lives. However, it's critical to keep in mind the difficulty of becoming God's disciples or stewards if we don't have a relationship of love based on both our will and our affection.

1. (a) In 1 Peter 4:7-11, Peter writes of being a "good stewards of the manifold grace of God." In your own words, explain how Peter would describe the responsibility of a steward.

   _____

   _____

   _____

   _____

   (b) What motivations for being a "good steward" do you discover from this passage?

   _____

   _____

   _____

   _____

2. (a) In Titus 1:7-9, Paul equates the office of overseer, or bishop, with the role of God's steward. How does Paul describe the responsibility of being God's steward?

   _____

   _____

   _____

   _____

(b) Why do you think Paul set such high standards?

_____

_____

_____

_____

(c) What, if any, are the implications of this passage for people who are not called to the role of overseer or bishop but who nevertheless desire to grow as disciples of Jesus?

_____

_____

_____

_____

3. (a) Stewardship is again addressed in 1 Corinthians 4:1-5. What connection is there between being "servants of Christ" and "stewards of the mysteries of God"?

_____

_____

_____

_____

(b) Paul says that a steward must be trustworthy. Give an example of what you think Paul means by "trustworthy."

_____

_____

_____

_____

(c) How does your dictionary define "trustworthy"?

_____

_____

_____

_____

(d) What principle(s) do you see regarding motivation for serving God?

_____

_____

_____

_____

> Jesus sometimes describes a disciple's life in terms of stewardship (cf. Matthew 25:14-30; Luke 12:42-48), not because being a steward is the whole of it but because this role sheds a certain light on it. An *oikonomos* or steward is one to whom the owner of a household turns over responsibility for caring for the property, managing affairs, making resources yield as much as possible, and sharing the resources with others. The position involves trust and accountability.
> —*Stewardship: A Disciple's Response*, National Conference of Catholic Bishops

4. (a) What areas of responsibility do you feel God has entrusted to you as a steward?

_____

_____

_____

_____

(b) What tensions, struggles, and pressures do you experience while fulfilling your responsibilities as a steward?

_____

_____

_____

_____

 Preparation for Session 3

1. Continue to read and mark your Bible daily, and record your thoughts in your prayer journal.

2. Complete questions 1-6 on "Jesus' Responsible Servant," pages 32-34.

Notes for Session 2

Notes for Session 2

Session 3

Jesus' Responsible Servant

▶ Before You Begin

Share insights from your prayer time and daily Bible reading.

Stewardship simply requires that we live responsibly with the resources, roles, and gifts God has given to us. First, we must be convinced that God has truly given us these gifts, and second, that he has designed us and our gifts to meet a need in his kingdom. Only when we recognize that we have been entrusted as stewards can we begin to responsibly fulfill this role.

Pope John Paul II makes several observations about responsibility:

> In the last analysis it seems to me that man's liberty is *what he discerns in himself when he feels responsible.* Obviously a certain discernment of liberty is bound up with this birth of awareness: "I have the choice". . . .
>
> Responsibility is not only knowledge. It comes into being at the point where knowledge passes to action. . . . Well then, responsibility indicates the necessity of acting in conformity with the known truth, that is, in accord with oneself, in accord with one's conscience and, to be more precise, with a conscience formed in the truth. Responsibility so understood is another name for moral obligation.
>
> —**Pope John Paul II** in *"Be Not Afraid!"*, pp. 99-100

As we reflect on the pope's words, it's readily apparent that "knowledge of the truth" and "a conscience formed in the truth" are prerequisites to being a responsible servant of Jesus. This focus on truth is one reason why sacred Scripture is so foundational to a disciple's life. Sacred

Scripture is necessary to really know truth. Consequently, it also is one of the reasons why we look to the Church for explanation of scriptural truths. We want to profit from the truth which God has communicated previously to his body and avoid falling into doctrinal error. Together, sacred Scripture and the Tradition of the Church help form our conscience. As you continue to discuss these scriptural truths about stewardship, remember to pray that your mind and heart, and subsequently your behavior, would be conformed more and more to Jesus.

1. (a) In Luke 12:35-48, Jesus teaches about faithfulness and then relates a parable about stewardship. Compare and contrast the characteristics of the faithful steward with those of the unfaithful steward.

_____

_____

_____

_____

(b) What motivation and rewards does Jesus give to encourage us to live responsibly as disciples?

_____

_____

_____

_____

(c) What are the concerns of the unfaithful steward?

_____

_____

_____

_____

2. (a) Jesus teaches another parable about stewardship in Matthew 25:14-30. Given that Jesus took time to tell such a prolonged story, how do you think he felt about the importance of being a responsible steward?

_____

_____

_____

_____

(b) What principle lesson(s) is Jesus trying to communicate to his disciples?

_____

_____

_____

_____

An amazing example of responsible stewardship took place in the life of a doctor living in Brighton, England, in the nineteenth century. As told by Mrs. Charles E. Cowman in *Streams in the Desert*, when stricken with blindness, Dr. William Moon prayed: "Lord, I accept this talent of blindness from you. Help me to use it for your glory, so that at your coming you receive your own with usury." The Lord granted him this prayer. He invented the Moon Alphabet, by which thousands of blind people were able to read the Bible.

3. How does Matthew 25:31-46 shed additional light on what Jesus means by investing our talents? What kinds of actions does Jesus want his stewards to take?

_____

_____

_____

_____

4. In 2 Corinthians 4:7-18, Paul identifies many possible reasons he could have used for not living as a responsible steward of Christ. Also within this passage are several reasons why he was motivated to serve Jesus and build the Church. What motivations or rationalizations do you see in this passage?

_____

_____

_____

_____

5. From these past two sessions, which motivations for stewardship do you find most challenging? Why?

_____

_____

_____

_____

6. (a) Jesus discusses what it means to be a servant in Mark 10:42-45. How does this passage affect your view of what it means to be a servant?

_____

_____

_____

_____

(b) Whom did Jesus serve? How did he serve them?

_____

_____

_____

_____

Without love, the outward work is of no value; but whatever is done out of love, be it never so little, is wholly fruitful. For God regards the greatness of the love that prompts a man, rather than the greatness of his achievement.

Whoever loves much, does much. Whoever does a thing well, does much. And he does well, who serves the community before his own interests.

—**Thomas á Kempis**, *The Imitation of Christ*, Book I, Chapter 15

 ## Preparation for Session 4

1. Continue to read and mark your Bible daily, and record your thoughts in your prayer journal.

2. Complete questions 1–7 on "Stewardship of Our Hearts," pages 40-45.

Notes for Session 3

Notes for Session 3

Session 4

Stewardship of Our Hearts

▶ Before You Begin

Share insights from your prayer time and daily Bible reading.

I n *Stewardship: A Disciple's Response,* the U.S. bishops state, "Being a disciple is not just something else to do, alongside many other things suitable for Christians; it is a total way of life and requires continuing conversion."

Conversion relates primarily to a change of heart. Our mind, will, and understanding are clearly involved, but one effect that we see and expect reflects a change in our deeply hidden affections—our spiritual, moral, and emotional center. This is why Jesus spoke frequently about issues of the heart. This is a focus of many other passages in Scripture as well.

> Conversion speaks of the change of heart that, as members of the Church, each one must undergo. The Gospel speaks across time and space to each human being, each mind, each heart. It asks us what we think about our lives, how we hope, whom we love, and what we live for. If faith is not transforming each heart and life, it is dead.
> —*Go and Make Disciples: A National Plan and Strategy for Catholic Evangelization in the United States,* National Conference of Catholic Bishops

Christian history is filled with individuals who were exceptional because their hearts were set on God. Mother Teresa of Calcutta, Ignatius of Loyola, Francis de Sales, Therese of Lisieux, Padre Pio, Pope John

XXIII—these are but a fraction of those who knew the change of heart that the gospel entails. These were people who gave God their hearts without reservation, who cultivated hearts responsive to God, and who served God with all their hearts. In reality, they were ordinary people like you and me who, with God's help, simply became stewards of their hearts in extraordinary ways.

1. The Scriptures use various adjectives to describe the spiritual conditions of the heart. Review some of these heart "conditions" from the following list. (Look up those passages that especially interest you.)

Brokenhearted	(Isaiah 61:1)
Hardness of heart	(Ephesians 4:18)
Cheerful heart	(Proverbs 17:22)
Honest and good heart	(Luke 8:15)
Contrite heart	(Psalm 51:17)
Merry heart	(Isaiah 24:7)
Dull heart	(Matthew 13:15)
Pure heart	(1 Timothy 1:5)
Evil and unbelieving heart	(Hebrews 3:12)
Sick heart	(Proverbs 13:12)
Fainthearted	(Isaiah 7:4)
Steadfast heart	(Psalm 108:1)
False heart	(Hosea 10:2)
Stouthearted	(Psalm 76:5)
Gentle and humble heart	(Matthew 11:29)
Stubborn heart	(Ezekiel 3:7)
Generous heart	(Acts 2:46)
True heart	(Hebrews 10:22)
Glad hearted	(Proverbs 15:13)
Willing heart	(Exodus 35:22)

(a) Which one characteristic would you most like to represent your future heart condition? Why? (You may also use other Scripture references.)

_____

_____

_____

_____

2. *The Catechism of the Catholic Church* states that its spiritual tradition "emphasizes the heart, in the biblical sense of the depths of one's being, where the person decides for or against God" (CCC, 368). Read Isaiah 29:13. What do you think the Lord meant by "their hearts are far from me"?

_____

_____

_____

_____

3. In Ezekiel 36:26, the Lord makes a promise to change the hearts of his people. Why would making sure we have a "heart of flesh" help us to be better stewards of our hearts than allowing ourselves to have "hearts of stone"? What are some ways that God fulfills his promise to change our hearts of stone into hearts of flesh?

_____

_____

_____

_____

4. In verse 23 of Proverbs 4:20-27, we are advised to "keep your heart with all vigilance, for from it flows the springs of life."

(a) What is the opposite of "keeping your heart"?

_____

_____

_____

_____

(b) What insights for "keeping your heart" do you see in this passage?

_____

_____

_____

_____

(c) What do the terms listed below mean to you?

"with all vigilance"

_____

_____

_____

_____

"flow the springs of life"

_____

_____

_____

_____

5. (a) According to Luke 6:43-45, why is it important as responsible stewards to safeguard the condition of our hearts?

_____

_____

_____

_____

(b) List, in order of priority, at least six practical ways you can store "good treasure" in your heart. Be prepared to explain why you put them in the order you did.

(1)_____   (4)_____

(2)_____   (5)_____

(3)_____   (6)_____

> All the Israelites did in fact leave the land of Egypt, but they did not all leave in so far as attachment to it was concerned. That is why, in the desert, many of them were sad that they did not have the onions and the meat of Egypt (Numbers 11:4-5). In the same way, there are penitents who in fact leave sin but do not leave their attachment to it.
> —St. Francis de Sales, *Introduction to the Devout Life*, Part I, Chapter 7

6. It is understandable why we might shrink back and try to cover up a sin in our hearts. What do the following passages tell us about the full disclosure of the condition of our hearts to God?

Luke 16:14-15:

_____

_____

_____

_____

Romans 8:26-27:

_____

_____

_____

_____

Hebrews 4:12-13:

_____

_____

_____

_____

The sacrament of Reconciliation enables us through self-examination to experience, first of all, disclosing our sins to ourselves, and secondly, disclosing our sins to a priest, who not only can pronounce forgiveness but who can also expedite healing.

> The confessor is not the master of God's forgiveness, but its servant. The minister of this sacrament should unite himself to the intention and charity of Christ. . . . and lead the penitent with patience toward healing and full maturity.
> —*Catechism of the Catholic Church*, 1466

> It is called the sacrament of Reconciliation, because it imparts to the sinner the love of God who reconciles: "Be reconciled to God." He who lives by God's merciful love is ready to respond to the Lord's call: "Go; first be reconciled to your brother."
> —*Catechism of the Catholic Church*, 1424

7. Based on the following passages, why should we have no fear about disclosing our hearts to God, even if we are feeling condemned or guilty?

1 John 3:18-22:

_____

_____

_____

_____

Hebrews 10:19-23:

_____

_____

_____

_____

Psalm 62:8:

_____

_____

_____

_____

Grant me, above all else, to rest in You, that my heart may find its peace in You alone; for You are the heart's true peace, its sole abiding place, and outside Yourself all is hard and restless. In this true peace that is in You, the sole, supreme, and eternal Good, I will dwell and take my rest. Amen.

—**Thomas à Kempis**, *The Imitation of Christ*, Book III, Chapter 15

 ## Preparation for Session 5

1. Continue to read and mark your Bible each day, and record your thoughts in your prayer journal.

2. Complete questions 1–5 on "Yielding Our Hearts to God," pages 52-56.

Notes for Session 4

Notes for Session 4

Notes for Session 4

Session 5

Yielding Our Hearts to God

▶ Before You Begin

Share insights from your prayer time and daily Bible reading.

As we study and discuss stewardship of our hearts, we realize how important and foundational it is to have a heart that is spiritually healthy. The wellspring of Christian spirituality is our inner life, of which these passages on the heart speak. In our desire to be people with integrity of heart—people whose hearts are wholly given over to the Lord in love—we must remember that our role as steward is one of cooperating with the Holy Spirit. It is God who brings about changes in our hearts and produces hearts that are tender and responsive to the Lord.

> The Prophets can preach the word, but they cannot bestow the Spirit. They speak most eloquently, but if You are silent, they cannot fire the heart. They instruct in the letter, but You open the understanding. They set forth the mysteries, but You reveal the meaning of all secrets. They teach your commandments, but You help us to observe them. They point the way, but You grant us strength to follow it. Their action is external; You instruct and enlighten the heart. They water the seed; You make it fruitful. They proclaim the words, but You impart understanding to the mind.
> —**Thomas à Kempis,** *The Imitation of Christ,* Book III, Chapter 2

We can be greatly encouraged by these words of Thomas á Kempis. God provides the means for change by providing the Holy Spirit. Our Father gives free reign to the Holy Spirit to work in our hearts to bring about the changes he desires. He simply asks that we not resist the Spirit, but instead cooperate with him. So as we continue our study and discussion, let's ask for the Holy Spirit's help. Together we will find both insight and strength to become successful stewards of our hearts.

1. (a) Psalm 51 mentions the heart three times. It prescribes several remedies for a heart that is estranged from God and that experiences guilt before him. What remedies do each of these passages suggest for dealing with guilt?

51:1-9:

_____

_____

_____

_____

51:10-14:

_____

_____

_____

_____

51:15-17:

_____

_____

_____

_____

(b) What practical means has God provided to:

"teach me wisdom in my secret heart"?

_____

_____

_____

_____

"Create in me a clean heart. . . and put a new and right spirit within me"?

_____

_____

_____

_____

(c) What does "a broken and contrite heart" mean to you?

_____

_____

_____

_____

One other name for the sacrament of Reconciliation used by the *Catechism of the Catholic Church* is the sacrament of conversion, "because it makes sacramentally present Jesus' call to conversion, the first step in returning to the Father from whom one has strayed by sin" (CCC, 1423). Fr. Henri J. M. Nouwen expressed it this way:

> Confession and forgiveness are precisely the disciplines by which spiritualization and carnality can be avoided and true incarnation lived. Through confession, the dark powers are taken out of their carnal isolation, brought into the light, and made visible. . . . Through forgiveness, they are disarmed and dispelled and a new integration between body and spirit is made possible.
> —**Henri J. M. Nouwen,** *In the Name of Jesus,* pp. 48-49

2. There are many positive actions we can take, and many negative actions we should avoid, to maintain a pure heart. In the following passages, identify what we can do to cooperate with the Holy Spirit. Then answer the questions pertaining to each passage.

Deuteronomy 6:4-9:

_____

_____

_____

_____

How do you keep this love for God in your heart?

_____

_____

_____

_____

Psalm 119:9-11:

_____

_____

_____

_____

What is the opposite of this behavior?

_____

_____

_____

_____

Proverbs 3:1-6:

_____

_____

_____

_____

Which concept in these verses seems most important to you?

_____

_____

_____

_____

Hebrews 10:16-18:

_____

_____

_____

_____

The author of Hebrews quotes the prophet Jeremiah, who promised that God will place his law in our hearts and write them on our minds. How are these two actions of God similar or different?

_____

_____

_____

_____

3. Mary is the best example of someone whose heart is fully yielded to the Lord. From Scripture (Luke 1:28-38; John 2:3-5, 19:25-27; and Acts 1:14) and your knowledge of Mary, how does she demonstrate this quality?

_____

_____

_____

_____

> Mary is above all the example of that worship that consists in making one's life an offering to God. . . . As she, anticipating in herself the wonderful petition of the Lord's Prayer—"Your will be done" (Matthew 6:10)—replied to God's messenger: "I am the handmaid of the Lord. Let what you have said be done to me" (Luke 1:38). And Mary's "yes" is for all Christians a lesson and example of obedience to the will of the Father, which is the way and means of one's own sanctification.
> —**Pope Paul VI**, *Marialis Cultus*, 20

4. Jesus is the perfect model of a heart fully yielded and obedient to the Father. In the Gospel of Matthew, Jesus describes his heart as gentle and humble. Read Matthew 11:28-29, Galatians 4:4-7, and Ephesians 3:14-19. Reflect on these passages, and then write a paragraph that expresses your understanding of hearts that are stewards of his grace.

   _____

   _____

   _____

   _____

5. If you were a "heart doctor"—caring for the spiritual condition of people's hearts—how would you diagnose yourself? What would you prescribe to ensure a spiritually healthy heart?

   _____

   _____

   _____

   _____

Holy Spirit of God: You inspired prophets and apostles
to speak and write in holy Scripture, and you constantly
illumine the hearts and mind of those who read.
Grant us a measure of inspiration and discernment in
our reading and writing, that we may discover truly who
we are and enter more fully into the nature and the love
of God, through Jesus Christ our Lord, Amen.
—**Brother Ramon SSF**, *Forty Days and Forty Nights*, p. 143

 Preparation for Session 6

1. Continue to read and mark your Bible daily, and record your
   thoughts in your prayer journal.

2. Complete questions 1–7 on "The Way in Which We Live:
   Our Time and Our Work," pages 62-67.

Notes for Session 5

Notes for Session 5

Session 6

The Way in Which We Live: Our Time and Our Work

Share insights from your prayer time and daily Bible reading.

We can think of stewardship as the practical result of discipleship. The root meaning of the words "disciple" and "discipleship" is a person who is a "learner." A disciple is someone who commits his life to learning about Christ and to living a disciplined life based on God's values and principles in order to honor and please him.

> As members of the Church, Jesus calls us to be disciples. This has astonishing implications:
> — Mature disciples make a conscious decision to follow Jesus, no matter what the cost.
> — Christian disciples experience conversion—life-shaping changes of mind and heart—and commit their very selves to the Lord.
> — Christian stewards respond in a particular way to the call to be a disciple. Stewardship has the power to shape and mold our understanding of our lives and the way in which we live.
> —*To Be a Christian Steward, A Summary of the U.S. Bishops' Pastoral Letter on Stewardship,* National Conference of Catholic Bishops

During these next two sessions, the phrase "the way in which we live"—taken from the above quote—will be our focus. Think about your daily life. Relationships, work, play, and possessions—all are part of our lives, and all represent the use of our time. Of course, we do not want to spend our lives foolishly. We want to invest them in living each day in a way that is pleasing to God. So let's begin by looking at values and principles that speak about investing our time.

Our Time

1. (a) Compare and contrast the way Christians are called to live with the way the nonbelievers were living as described in Ephesians 4:17-24.

   _____

   _____

   _____

   _____

   (b) Based on this passage, describe the cause-and-effect relationship illustrated by these examples. How do our minds and thoughts ultimately lead to either good or bad actions?

   _____

   _____

   _____

   _____

2. The Bible, and especially St. Paul's letters, are filled with practical advice on how to live as a disciple of Jesus. What principles for Christ-like behavior do you find in Ephesians 5:8-20?

   _____

   _____

   _____

   _____

3. Paul was not interested in time because he was overly efficient or particularly concerned about time management. What was Paul's real concern, as indicated by Colossians 4:2-6 and Ephesians 5:15-17?

   _____

   _____

   _____

   _____

> So teach us to count our days that we may gain a wise heart.
> —**Psalm 90:12**

> Always remember your end, and that lost time never returns.
> —**Thomas á Kempis**, *The Imitation of Christ*, Book I, Chapter 25

We spend much time interacting with others. Christ's concern for us is that we should extend his gospel of love and compassion to others rather than allowing any sinful influences from others to draw us away from Christ.

> By reason of their special vocation it belongs to the laity to seek the kingdom of God by engaging in temporal affairs and directing them according to God's will. They live in the world, that is, they are engaged in each and every work and business of the earth and in the ordinary circumstances of social and family life which, as it were, constitute their very existence. There they are called by God that, being led by the spirit to the Gospel, they may contribute to the sanctification of the world, as from within like leaven, by fulfilling their own particular duties. Thus, especially by the witness of their life, resplendent in faith, hope, and charity, they must manifest Christ to others.
> —**Vatican II**, *Dogmatic Constitution on the Church*, 31

4. What do the following verses teach us about our relationships with others?

Mark 2:15-17:

_____

_____

_____

_____

Proverbs 4:13-15, 18-19:

_____

_____

_____

_____

Luke 10:30-37:

_____

_____

_____

_____

> Jesus gradually reveals the characteristics and demands of the kingdom through his words, his actions and his own person. . . . The kingdom aims at transforming human relationships; it grows gradually as people slowly learn to love, forgive and serve one another. Jesus sums up the whole Law, focusing it on the commandment of love.
> —**Pope John Paul II**, *Mission of the Redeemer*, 14

5. (a) Much of our time also should be invested in relating to the family of God, the body of Christ. While we cannot possibly discuss all the passages describing how we should relate to other Christians, identify the principles emphasized in the following three passages.

Colossians 3:12-15:

_____

_____

_____

Galatians 6:1-5:

_____

_____

_____

Galatians 6:7-10:

_____

_____

_____

(b) Which of these principles do you believe is the most difficult for a disciple to follow?

_____

_____

_____

Our Work

The New Testament knows no distinction between the "sacred," over which Christ has control, and the "secular," which is up for grabs. Instead, Christ expects us to live all of our lives under His lordship. . . .

> As a Christian, then, you have more reason than most to view your daily work as profoundly significant. You are a servant of Christ, and He is using you and your work to accomplish His purposes. . . .
>
> Therefore, everything about our jobs should be directed toward Him—our purpose and motives, our profits and their use, our decisions, our problems, our relationships with coworkers and customers, our plans, our goals, our equipment, our financing—*everything.*
> —**Doug Sherman** and **William Hendricks**, *Your Work Matters to God*, p. 114-115

6. (a) Many people today spend the majority of their time working at their jobs and caring for their families. Yet somehow everything we do in our lives should glorify God. Read Matthew 22:36-37 and Colossians 3:17. What do these passages teach us about what our attitude should be in every activity in our lives?

   _____

   _____

   _____

   _____

(b) Why do you think God cares about the "way in which we live" when it comes to our jobs?

_____

_____

_____

_____

7. (a) What further insight does Philippians 2:12-15 provide for how we are to live our lives, even at work?

_____

_____

_____

_____

(b) What motivations can you discover in these verses for living life with a positive attitude, free of complaining?

_____

_____

_____

_____

 ## Preparation for Session 7

1. Continue to read and mark your Bible daily, and record your thoughts in your prayer journal.

2. Complete questions 1-10 on "The Way in Which We Live: Our Finances and Our Words," pages 72-77.

Notes for Session 6

Notes for Session 6

Session 7

The Way in Which We Live: Our Finances and Our Words

▶ Before You Begin

Share insights from your prayer time and daily Bible reading.

Perhaps two of the clearest indicators of our discipleship, or the "way in which we live," are the use of our finances and material possessions, and the ideas, attitudes, and concerns expressed in our speech. As we will see in this study, Jesus draws a connection between the treasures of our heart and how we use our money. Jesus also draws a connection between the state of our hearts and the words that come out of our mouth.

For some of us, the key to aligning our words and finances with the Father's desires will involve a change of heart and the things stored there. For others, it will simply involve a growing understanding of his will, which will help us to make the necessary adjustments.

> What identifies a steward? Safeguarding material and human resources and using them responsibly are one answer; so is generous giving of time, talent, and treasure. But being a Christian steward means more. As Christian stewards, we receive God's gifts gratefully, cultivate them responsibly, share them lovingly in justice with others, and return them with increase to the Lord.
> —*To Be a Christian Steward, A Summary of the U.S. Bishops' Pastoral Letter on Stewardship*, National Conference of Catholic Bishops

Our finances and our words can be important means for expressing our love for God. God also may use these areas to express through us his love for others. As disciples we have an important responsibility. This session offers an opportunity to consider and discuss the implications of being a disciple with our finances and through our speech.

Our Money

1. (a) What, in your opinion, is the message Jesus teaches in Matthew 6:19-21?

_____

_____

_____

_____

   (b) How does a person "store up treasures in heaven"?

_____

_____

_____

_____

2. How does St. Paul's advice in 1 Timothy 6:17-19 guide Christians who are financially well-off to use their money?

_____

_____

_____

_____

3. (a) When St. Paul talks about the proper attitude toward money in 1 Timothy 6:6-10, what are the primary truths he communicates?

_____

_____

_____

_____

(b) Having read Paul's warnings regarding wealth (1 Timothy 6: 9-10) and his encouragement to the affluent Christians (6:18-19), describe a balanced attitude toward money.

_____

_____

_____

_____

4. (a) Jesus also taught his disciples how God views money when he saw a poor widow in the temple. What important conclusions does Jesus make from this incident in Mark 12:41-44?

_____

_____

_____

_____

(b) What factors should govern our support of the Church?

_____

_____

_____

_____

Our Divine Lord was interested in studying the alms-givers, and it was the quality of their giving which arrested Him far more than the quantity they gave. . . . Probably the poor woman at the temple did not see her Judge or know that she had pleased Him, or guess that, in the scales of Divine Justice, she gave more than all those others who put offerings into the treasury. They gave of their superfluity: she gave all she had, "her whole livelihood." She was poor, yet she gave to the poor. She emptied herself to fill the emptiness of others. The jingle of her two small coins as they fell cried out to refute the whole base philosophy of materialism, which would teach men to acquire as much as they can—as if this earth were our only home.

—**Fulton J. Sheen**, *On Being Human*, p. 152

5. God has called each of us to be his trustworthy stewards. What trustworthy uses for money do the following passages suggest?

Matthew 25:37-40:

_____

_____

_____

_____

Acts 20:33-35:

_____

_____

_____

_____

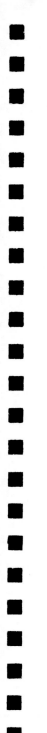

1 Corinthians 9:8-14:

_____

_____

_____

_____

James 2:14-17:

_____

_____

_____

_____

6. In 2 Corinthians 9, St. Paul discusses some important truths about generosity. See how many principles you can discover. Which do you find the most challenging? Explain why this truth is important.

_____

_____

_____

_____

Our Speech

7. (a) In Matthew 12:33-37, Jesus links our speech with the desires of our hearts. What do you think he meant by "good things" and "evil things" (12:35)?

_____

_____

_____

_____

(b) How do we fill the "abundance of the heart" (12:34) with good things?

_____

_____

_____

_____

8. James' letter also draws a correlation between our speech and what is in our hearts (1:26-27; 3:1-12). Why is it important to control the tongue?

_____

_____

_____

_____

9. The tongue can be used for great good or great evil. Reflect on the elements of positive Christian speech in the following three chapters of Proverbs: 10:18-21; 12:17-19,22; 15:1,4,22-23,28. After thinking about these verses, develop six guidelines for positive Christian speech.

(1)_____

(2)_____

(3)_____

(4)_____

(5)_____

(6)_____

> Truthfulness, simplicity and sincerity in speech are a great ornament to Christian life. David said: "I said, I will guard against my ways not to sin with my tongue." "Set a watch, Lord, at my mouth, at the door which closes my lips" (Psalms 39:1; 141:3).
> —St. Francis de Sales, *Introduction to the Devout Life*, Part III, Chapter 30

10. Take a few minutes to review the material you studied in sessions six and seven. How might God be calling you as a steward to serve him better with your time, in your relationships, with your finances, and through your words?

_____

_____

_____

_____

 Preparation for Session 8

1. Continue to read and mark your Bible daily, and record your thoughts in your prayer journal.

2. Complete questions 1–5 on "Entrusted with Jesus' Mission," pages 82-86.

Notes for Session 7

Notes for Session 7

Session 8

Entrusted with Jesus' Mission

▶ Before You Begin

Share insights from your prayer time and daily Bible reading.

Jesus was sent on a mission from his Father. His mission was to establish the kingdom of God—or the reign of God—in the world and in the lives of people. His Spirit now offers God's kingdom to all humanity. The kingdom of God paves the way for a new relationship with the Father, through Jesus, as the Holy Spirit dwells in us. This is the gospel, the "Good News" of the kingdom. In his last days on earth, Jesus set his face like flint toward the climatic conclusion of his mission: his death and resurrection. And when he uttered from the cross, "It is finished," died, and then rose from the dead and ascended to the Father, his mission was completed. During those final weeks before and after his resurrection, Jesus entrusted to his followers the responsibility and opportunity for spreading the Good News of the kingdom through their lives and words.

So, where does that leave us, today's followers of Jesus? Perhaps these words of Pope Paul VI will provide a fitting introduction to answering this question:

> Those who sincerely accept the Good News, through the power of this acceptance and of shared faith, therefore gather together in Jesus' name in order to seek together the kingdom, build it up and live it. They make up a community which is in its turn evangelizing. The command to the Twelve to go out and proclaim the Good News is also valid for all Christians, though in a different way. . . . Those who have received the Good News and who have been gathered by it into the community of salvation can and must communicate and spread it. . . .

Finally, the person who has been evangelized goes on to evangelize others. Here lies the test of truth, the touchstone of evangelization: it is unthinkable that a person should accept the Word and give himself to the kingdom without becoming a person who bears witness to it and proclaims it in his turn.

—**Pope Paul VI**, *On Evangelization in the Modern World*, 14, 15

1. Restate in your own words the mission of Jesus as he introduced it in Luke 4:16-21 and 4:42-44.

   _____

   _____

   _____

   _____

2. (a) Listed below are five passages in which Jesus entrusts his mission to his disciples or "stewards." In each passage, how does Jesus urge these first disciples to carry out their mission?

   Matthew 28:16-20:

   _____

   _____

   _____

   _____

   Mark 16:14-16:

   _____

   _____

   _____

   _____

Luke 24:44-49:

_____

_____

_____

_____

John 20:19-23:

_____

_____

_____

_____

Acts 1:6-8:

_____

_____

_____

_____

(b) In the passages above, what motivation and encouragement did Jesus provide to fulfill this mission?

_____

_____

_____

_____

3. According to the following passages, why is the proclamation of the "Good News" of Jesus' kingdom so essential?

Acts 4:10-12:

_____

_____

_____

_____

Romans 8:1-4:

_____

_____

_____

_____

Romans 10:14-17:

_____

_____

_____

_____

1 Timothy 2:1-7:

_____

_____

_____

_____

4. How do you understand this mission for your own life? What role do you think that the Lord may be calling you to fill so that you can participate in his mission?

_____

_____

_____

_____

> If we go back to the beginnings of the Church, we find a clear affirmation that Christ is the one Savior of all, the only one able to reveal God and lead to God. In reply to the Jewish religious authorities who question the apostles about the healing of the lame man, Peter says: "By the name of Jesus Christ of Nazareth whom you crucified, whom God raised from the dead, by him this man is standing before you well. . . . And there is salvation in no one else, for there is no other name under heaven given among men by which we must be saved" (Acts 4:10,12). This statement, which was made to the Sanhedrin, has a universal value, since for all people—Jews and Gentiles alike—salvation can only come from Jesus Christ.[1]
> —**Pope John Paul II**, *Mission of the Redeemer*, 5

5. (a) St. Paul successfully shared the gospel and established a Christian community among the believers in Thessalonica. Read 1 Thessalonians 1:1-9; 2:1-10. In your own words, explain the reasons why you think St. Paul and those who preached with him were able to win these people to faith in Jesus.

_____

_____

_____

_____

(b) What did St. Paul and his companions avoid doing that might have caused setbacks in their efforts to evangelize?

_____

_____

_____

_____

[1] For a more thorough understanding of salvation as it relates to non-Christians, read *On Evangelization in the Modern World,* section 53, by Pope Paul VI; and *Mission of the Redeemer,* sections 4-7, by Pope John Paul II.

Preparation for Session 9

1. Continue to read and mark your Bible daily, and record your thoughts in your prayer journal.

2. Complete questions 1-6 on "Ambassadors for Christ," pages 92-95.

Notes for Session 8

Notes for Session 8

Notes for Session 8

Session 9

Ambassadors
for Christ

▶ Before You Begin

Share insights from your prayer time and daily Bible reading.

The words "evangelism" and "evangelization" often generate a chill of apprehension because of the misuse and misconceptions surrounding these terms. We could liberate ourselves from these fears if we realized that personal witness is merely a friend telling a friend about another friend. If the things we tell about our friend Jesus are true, people often will respond, "Your friend Jesus sounds like a wonderful person. I wish I could meet him." This is the way personal witness should be—not high-pressured persuasion, but genuine conversation about a real, wonderful person who loves us and has saved us.

Sometimes our fear may come from the contradiction that we know exists between the way we live and the message we bring. As Pope Paul VI noted, we are right to sense a vital connection between the two:

> For the Church, the first means of evangelization is the witness of an authentically Christian life, given over to God in a communion that nothing should destroy and at the same time given to one's neighbor with limitless zeal. As we said recently to a group of lay people, "Modern man listens more willingly to witnesses than to teachers, and if he does listen to teachers, it is because they are witnesses." . . . It is therefore primarily by her conduct and by her life that the Church will evangelize the world, in other words, by her living witness of fidelity to the Lord Jesus.
> —**Pope Paul VI**, *On Evangelization in the Modern World,* 41

The joy, peace, purpose, and compassion that should flow from our relationship with Christ attract people to us and make them wonder why our lives seem different and more meaningful. These qualities also bring the gospel to those around us. This is why the way we live is crucial to evangelization. Our joy, our love, and our peace set the groundwork to share the reason for the hope within us. Our lives are the evidence that this message of hope we bring is credible. Both are essential—the witness of how we live and a willingness to share with others the Good News of Jesus.

> The Good News proclaimed by the witness of life sooner or later has to be proclaimed by the word of life. There is no true evangelization if the name, the teaching, the life, the promises, the kingdom and the mystery of Jesus of Nazareth, the Son of God, are not proclaimed.
> —**Pope Paul VI**, *On Evangelization in the Modern World*, 22

1. Read 1 Peter 2:9. What "mighty acts" of God have you seen in your own life? What might be appealing about these acts of God to your friends who may not believe in Christ?

   _____

   _____

   _____

   _____

2. (a) According to 1 Peter 3:13–18, what are three important ways to share the gospel with people whose faith seems weak or nonexistent?

   _____

   _____

   _____

   _____

(b) How does 1 Peter 3:13-18 change your perspective on experiencing mistreatment even when you are trying to do something good, or even when you are sharing "an accounting for the hope that is in you" (3:15)?

_____

_____

_____

_____

3. Based on Philippians 2:14-15, describe the kind of behavior that will cause us to stand out like a brilliant light in a dark world.

_____

_____

_____

_____

4. (a) Identify the role and responsibility St. Paul says we have as Christians in 2 Corinthians 5:14—6:2.

_____

_____

_____

_____

(b) What does "reconciliation" mean to you?

_____

_____

_____

_____

(c) What are the responsibilities of an ambassador?

_____

_____

_____

_____

(d) How do you feel about being Jesus' ambassador to family and friends who may not know Christ?

_____

_____

_____

_____

5. (a) If you could read the message of reconciliation contained in 2 Corinthians 5:17–6:2 to a friend whose faith seems weak, what points would you underscore?

_____

_____

_____

_____

(b) Which benefits of reconciliation might be most appealing to acquaintances and friends whose faith in Christ has not yet been awakened?

_____

_____

_____

_____

> The Holy Spirit is the fire of Jesus. The Spirit, the first gift of the risen Christ to his people, gives us both the ability to receive the Gospel of Jesus and, in response, the power to proclaim it. Without the Holy Spirit, evangelization simply cannot occur. The Spirit brings about evangelization in the life of the Church and in the Church's sharing the Gospel with others.
>
> *—Go and Make Disciples: A National Plan and Strategy for Catholic Evangelization in the United States*, National Conference of Catholic Bishops

6. St. Paul writes a beautiful description of his mission, and his stewardship of it, in Colossians 1:24-29. How can you incorporate Paul's description of his mission to enhance your own commitment to be a steward of the mission?

_____

_____

_____

_____

Conclusion

Congratulations! Like all good stewards, you have used your time and energy well by investing it to draw closer to Christ and to become a better disciple. It is not by accident that you have done so. The Holy Spirit has led you into this process of discovery. He has done this so that, with his help, you can bear much fruit in the kingdom of God. We pray that God will honor you for your effort and use you for his service and glory. God bless you!

Acknowledgments (continued from page 5)

Quotations on pages 17 and 31 from *"Be Not Afraid!" Pope John Paul II Speaks Out on His Life, His Beliefs, and His Inspiring Vision for Humanity*, by André Frossard, translated from the French by Jr. R. Foster, St. Martin's Press, New York, 1984.

Quotations on pages 23 and 26 from *Stewardship: A Disciple's Response: A Pastoral Letter on Stewardship*, National Conference of Catholic Bishops, Washington, D.C., 1993.

Quotations on pages 35, 46, 51, and 63 from *The Imitation of Christ*, by Thomas á Kempis, Dorset Press, New York, 1986.

Quotations on pages 39 and 95 from *Go and Make Disciples: A National Plan and Strategy for Catholic Evangelization in the United States*, National Conference of Catholic Bishops, Washington, D.C., November 18, 1992.

Quotations on pages 43 and 76 from *Introduction to the Devout Life*, by St. Francis de Sales, S.F.S. Publications, Bangalore, India, 1990.

Quotation on page 53 from *In the Name of Jesus, Reflections on Christian Leadership*, by Henri J. M. Nouwen, The Crossroad Publishing Co., New York, 1989.

Quotation on page 56 from Apostolic Exhortation of Pope Paul VI for the Right Ordering and Development of Devotion to the Blessed Virgin Mary (*Marialis Cultus*), issued February 2, 1974.

Quotation on page 57 from *Forty Days and Forty Nights, A Guide to Spending Time Alone with God*, by Brother Ramon SSF, HarperCollins Publishers, 1993.

Quotations on pages 61 and 71 from *To Be a Christian Steward, A Summary of the U.S. Bishops' Pastoral Letter on Stewardship*, National Conference of Catholic Bishops, Washington, D.C., 1993.

Quotation on page 63 from the Second Vatican Council, *Dogmatic Constitution on the Church* (*Lumen Gentium*), issued November 21, 1964.

Quotations on pages 5, 14, 64, and 85 from *Mission of the Redeemer*, Encyclical Letter of Pope John Paul II (*Redemptoris Missio*), issued December 7, 1990.

Quotation on page 66 from *Your Work Matters to God*, Doug Sherman and William Hendricks, NavPress, Colorado Springs, Colorado, 1987.

Quotation on page 74 from O*n Being Human, Reflections on Life and Living*, by Fulton J. Sheen, Doubleday, New York, 1982.

Quotations on pages 82, 91, and 92 from Apostolic Exhortation of Pope Paul VI on *Evangelization in the Modern World* (*Evangelii Nuntiandi*), issued December 8, 1975.

Notes

Notes

Notes

Notes

About the Author

Rich Cleveland and his wife Gail have been involved in ministry since 1974. Rich has served in several leadership positions at Holy Apostles Parish in Colorado Springs, Colorado, including as director of the Small Christian Communities Ministry for the past seven years. He and his wife have three grown children.

Rich also is director of Emmaus Journey: Catholic Small Group Ministry. Through this ministry, Rich and Gail have published several Scripture-based Catholic small group studies. Additionally, Rich publishes *Reflecting on Sunday's Readings*, a small group study based on each Sunday's Mass readings, which can be downloaded for free from the Emmaus Journey Web site at www.emmausjourney.org.

Rich has served as speaker and seminar leader at numerous national Christian conferences and conventions, including the Franciscan University of Steubenville's Men's Conference, the National Council of Catholic Evangelization, and St. Paul's Institute of Evangelical Catholic Ministry.

Also by Rich Cleveland

Learn from Scripture about the way of prayer, conversion, and faith from these Bible studies. The workbook-type format can help individuals seeking to understand Scripture, spouses who want to grow together in their faith, or Bible study groups.

Each Bible Study features:
- Solid Catholic understanding
- Questions for thought or discussion
- Important Scripture passages for each topic
- Plenty of room to write

Embracing the Kingdom: A Bible Study on Conversion

This study will lay a strong foundation for prayer, conversion, faith, and growing as a member of the body of Christ.

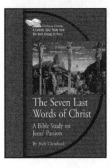

The Seven Last Words of Christ: A Bible Study on Jesus' Passion

The Seven Last Words of Christ will help you to meditate and pray with Jesus as he endured the agony of the cross. Learn to pray with Jesus, "Father, forgive them . . ." and hear his comforting words, "Today, you will be with me in Paradise."

Stop by and see us as you journey on the Web

Emmaus Journey: Catholic Evangelization and Discipleship through small groups provides Scripture-based resources and foundational training in Catholic spirituality

On the Emmaus Journey web page, small group studies are *free* to download and reproduce for use in your parish. You will find additional small group resources and free downloads to assist you in your small group ministry.

In addition, at *The Word Among Us* web page, we offer *free of charge* –
- the Scripture readings used at Mass for each day
- daily meditations and reflections based on the Mass readings
- practical articles on Christian living
- reviews of the newest Emmaus Journey Bible Studies

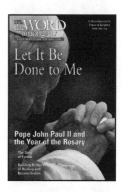

Please visit our websites today!

Emmaus Journey
www.emmausjourney.org
email: info@emmausjourney.org
phone: 719-599-0448

www.wordamongus.org
email: theresa@wau.org
phone: 800-775-9673